W9-ALL-994

Nature CLOSE-UPS Nature

Flutter By,
Butterfly

-Text and photographs by Densey Clyne-

Gareth Stevens Publishing
MILWAUKEE

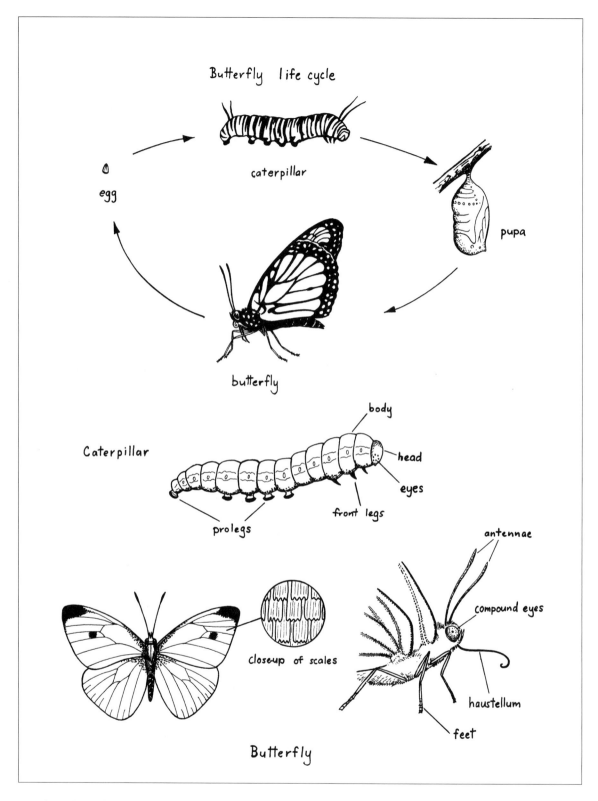

Words that appear in the glossary are printed in **boldface** type the first time they occur in the text.

Tailed emperor

Have you ever seen a purple moonbeam, a painted lady, or a tailed emperor? It is possible that you have. These are the common names of some butterflies.

Beautiful butterfly names

Monarch

Butterflies sometimes have different names in different places. This butterfly (*above*) is known as a monarch in the United States, its original home. In some other parts of the world, such as Australia, it is called the wanderer. The monarch is also known as the milkweed butterfly because its **caterpillars** feed on plants in the milkweed family.

A blue triangle feeds on a daisy.

Blue triangles are welcome visitors to any garden. At one time, they were called blue sailors because their wings are shaped like sails. They were also called blue fanny — a name they were given long ago when *Fanny* was a popular girl's name.

The beautiful names of butterflies show how much they are admired.

Orchard swallowtail caterpillar

Caterpillars look quite different from butter-flies. The orchard swallowtail caterpillar (*above*) looks sort of like bird droppings. This disguise helps it survive.

Without caterpillars, there would not be any butterflies or moths. At the beginning of its life, the butterfly caterpillar eats and grows. When the time is right, it changes into its adult form — a butterfly!

Butterfly eggs

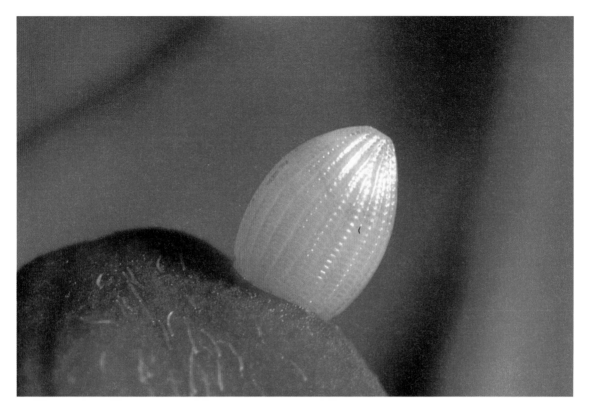

Monarch egg on a milkweed plant

The first stage in a butterfly's life is the egg.
Some butterfly **species** lay eggs in groups.
Others, like the monarch, lay just one egg at
a time. A monarch egg (*above*) is no bigger than
the head of a pin.

Most caterpillars eat the leaves of only
certain plants. So the mother lays her eggs on
or near the plants she knows the young will like
to eat.   Monarchs lay eggs on milkweeds.

Hatching, feeding, and growing

A birdwing caterpillar feeds on its own eggshell.

For its first meal, a newly hatched birdwing caterpillar eats the shell of the egg from which it came. From then on, the caterpillar eats only leaves. It will grow quickly. A caterpillar's main job is to eat!

A caterpillar grows a lot before it reaches the next stage of life. It **molts**, or sheds its skin, four or five times during its life. Each time, it replaces the old skin with new.

A birdwing caterpillar after molting

Before molting, a caterpillar stops feeding for a day or so and produces a special kind of molting fluid. This fluid softens the old skin and separates it from the new one. The old skin then splits at the head. The caterpillar "works" the skin backward off its body. The new skin stays stretchy for a short time so the caterpillar can expand into it. Some caterpillars look quite different after molting.

Special equipment

Close-up of an orchard swallowtail caterpillar

The little round eyes of the caterpillar — six on each side — do not see very well. In fact, they can only tell light from dark. A caterpillar finds food through its sense of smell. It smells and tastes with tiny hairlike sensors on its **antennae** and mouthparts.

Caterpillars have three pairs of legs at the front of their bodies. Behind these legs are five pairs of shorter legs called **prolegs**.

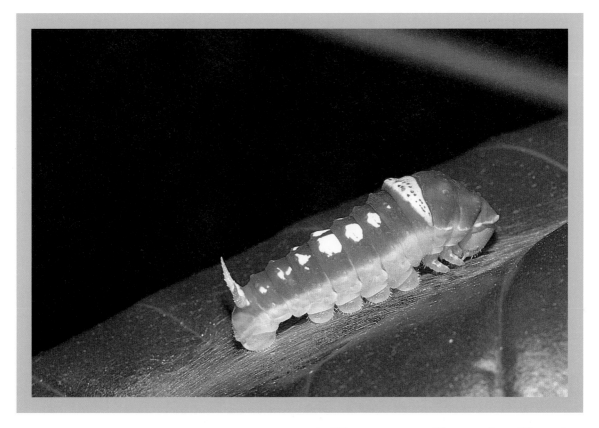

A Ulysses caterpillar on its silk pad

A caterpillar's prolegs are really suction disks with sets of tiny hooks on them.

This Ulysses caterpillar *(above)* has woven a silk pad on a leaf. It will rest on this pad and digest its food. The hooks act like Velcro to help latch the caterpillar to the silk. When the caterpillar moves around, the hooks secure it to rough surfaces. The suction disks give it a foothold on smooth surfaces.

Enemies and defenses

An assassin bug attacks a lacewing caterpillar.

A caterpillar has many enemies, such as birds and insects, that would like to eat it. The assassin bug has a dagger instead of a mouth. In the picture (*above*), it is attacking a lacewing caterpillar with its dagger.

Caterpillars use a variety of techniques to protect themselves from **predators**. Some use **camouflage**, while others have built-in chemical defenses against their enemies.

Ants protect a caterpillar in return for honeydew.

These ants look as if they are carrying off a caterpillar to their nest for dinner. But they are not attacking it — they are just riding piggyback. Caterpillars have friendly relationships with some kinds of ants. The ants drink the sweet honeydew produced by the caterpillars.

In return for the honeydew, the ants protect the caterpillars against enemies.

A caterpillar pupates

Orchard swallowtail preparing to pupate

Pupa completely formed

Butterflies go through **metamorphosis**, or changes in shape. When the caterpillar sheds its final skin, it stops moving and feeding. The orchard swallowtail caterpillar in the *top* picture is ready for the **pupa** stage of insect metamorphosis.

In the *bottom* picture, its skin now forms a protective shell called a **chrysalis**. Its tail hooks onto a plant, and it rests in a silk sling for safety. It is now in the pupa stage.

*Monarch
butterfly pupa*

Look closely to see the eyes, antennae, mouthparts, and wings of this monarch butterfly-to-be. Inside its body, organs for digesting **nectar** and muscles to move its wings are developing. If it is a female, it must be able to produce eggs. Although the pupa is quite still, it is very much alive.

A butterfly gets its wings

A red lacewing is getting its wings.

Opposite: A red lacewing fully emerged

A red lacewing butterfly emerges from the chrysalis (*above*). Its wings, packed tightly inside the chrysalis for weeks, will soon expand to their full size (*opposite*).

A Union Jack has emerged from the chrysalis beside it.

All butterflies have four wings, two on each side, that move together in flight as one. The wings of this newly emerged Union Jack butterfly are in perfect condition. By the end of the butterfly's life, they will be scratched and battered, perhaps even torn and broken.

Tiny scales cover a butterfly's wings and body. They are not tough and clear like the scales on a fish. The scales are loose and easily rub off.

Common eggfly

The Union Jack and most other butterflies get their vivid color patterns from **pigments** in their wing scales. Some butterflies seem to change color when viewed from different positions. This is due to tiny structures on the wing scales that break up the light.

This male common eggfly butterfly (*above*) has blue and white patches on its wings. But from a different angle, the blue disappears and only the white patches are visible.

A butterfly eats by drinking

A *skipper butterfly feeds*.

Caterpillars eat leaves, but butterflies feed on the nectar of flowers. They draw the nectar up through a long, slender tube called the **proboscis**. The tube contains taste sensors. This skipper butterfly (*above*) probes deeply into the nectar at the base of a tiny flower.

Close-up of butterfly's head

Three things are necessary for a butterfly's survival — the proboscis, eyes, and antennae.

The proboscis is barely visible here, coiled up while the butterfly rests. Two prominent, compound eyes allow the butterfly to see in all directions at once. They help the butterfly recognize predators and food. The antennae help the butterfly detect scents. But it is the color and shapes of flowers and other butterflies that attract attention long before a butterfly is able to detect any scent.

A butterfly feeds on a daisy.

Butterflies need flowers for food as much as flowers need butterflies to **pollinate** them. Some flowers are in the shape of a narrow tube, making it easy for butterflies to drink from them. Butterflies particularly like flowers in the daisy family. Tiny cups of nectar lie in the center of daisies. A butterfly can rest comfortably there while it feeds. Purple, pink, and blue flowers attract the most butterflies. Swallowtails and monarchs prefer red flowers.

On guard for enemies

A crab spider attacks
a painted lady.

Spiders, birds, lizards, and certain insects **prey** on butterflies. Crab spiders lurk in flowers to ambush butterflies. Other predators snatch and grab. Birds probably catch more butterflies than any of the other predators.

A monarch cater-pillar feeds on a plant in the milkweed family.

Monarch caterpillars feed on plants of the milkweed family. The milky sap in the leaves contains poisons that do not harm the caterpillars. It can be a lifesaver, in fact, because the poisons stay in a caterpillar's body and make the little creature taste horrible to predators.

The poison passes from the caterpillar to the adult butterfly. So hungry predators, such as birds, are certain to avoid eating monarchs!

Monarch butterfly

Butterflies as winged messengers

The male birdwing (right) *has brighter colors than the female.*

Wing colors and patterns play a big part in the way butterflies recognize each other and communicate. Soon after emerging from its chrysalis, the brightly colored male birdwing marks out a territory and waits for a suitable **mate**. He chases away other male birdwings, other types of butterflies, and even small birds — in fact, anything that is the wrong shape or color. Only a female of his own kind is welcome.

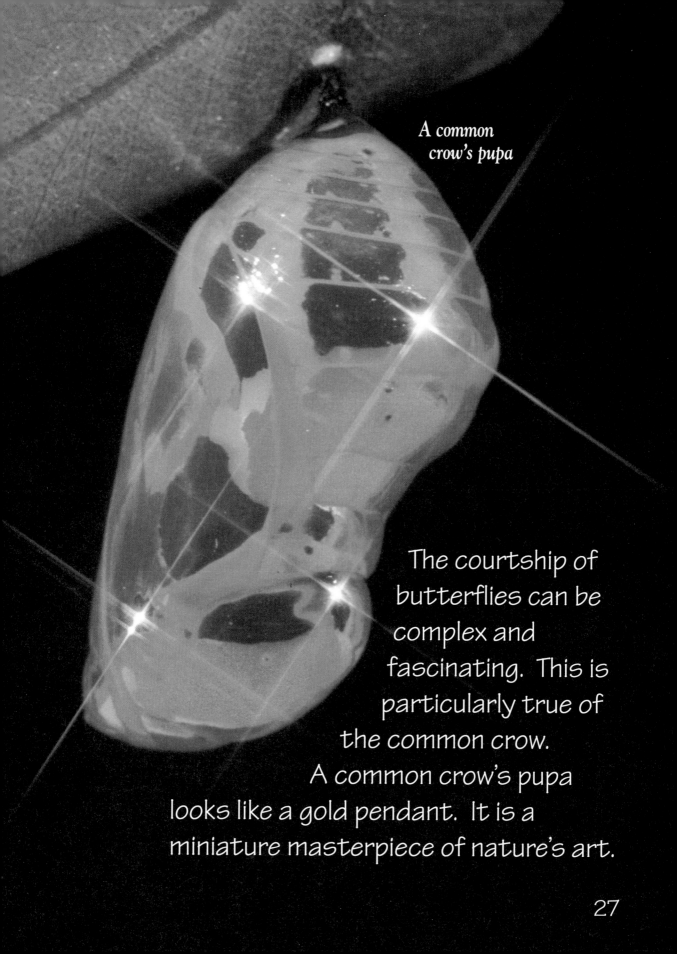

A common
crow's pupa

The courtship of
butterflies can be
complex and
fascinating. This is
particularly true of
the common crow.
A common crow's pupa
looks like a gold pendant. It is a
miniature masterpiece of nature's art.

Male common crow's hair pencils

Once a male common crow has been chosen by a female, he settles into a flight pattern close above her. When the time is right, he suddenly produces from a pocket in the tip of his body two spectacular yellow-gold, brushlike objects. These are called hair pencils. He hovers close above the female, waving these brushes, and showers her with fragments of the scented golden hairs. He also beats his wings so that his special scent is detected by sensors on her antennae. If she responds to his messages with the right signals, they mate.

Green spotted triangle

Most butterflies survive for only a few weeks, although the monarch lives for six months or more. The adult butterfly's role is to produce a new generation. After mating, the female butterfly lays her eggs.

When her caterpillars hatch, they are surrounded by plenty of food until they are ready to pupate. Then one day, they emerge as beautiful, winged butterflies. Encourage butterflies to visit your home by planting as many flowers as you can.

Ulysses butterfly

Glossary

antennae: a pair of thin, movable organs on the head of insects and other animals. Antennae are used for touching and smelling.

camouflage: a way of disguising something or someone to make it look like its surroundings.

caterpillar: the worm-like larva of a moth or butterfly.

chrysalis: the pupa of a butterfly.

mate (*n*): the male or female of a pair of animals.

metamorphosis: a complete change in appearance or form.

molt: to shed an outer covering.

nectar: the sweet liquid produced by flowers that attracts bees, birds, and other animals.

pigment: a substance in animal or plant tissue that gives it coloration.

pollinate: to place spores called pollen on a plant.

predator: an animal that hunts other animals for food.

prey (*v*): to hunt an animal for food.

proboscis: the elongated organ of a butterfly that is used for drinking nectar.

prolegs: pairs of legs on the bodies of some insect larvae.

pupa: the stage in the life of an insect when it is changing from a larva into an adult.

species: a group of beings with similar characteristics that are of the same type and that mate together.

Books to Read

Butterflies. The New Creepy Crawly Collection (series). Graham Coleman (Gareth Stevens)

Butterflies: Magical Metamorphosis. Secrets of the Animal World (series). Eulalia García (Gareth Stevens)

Butterflies and Moths. John Feltwell (Eyewitness Explorers)

Butterfly and Moth. Paul Whalley (Knopf)

A Closer Look at Butterflies. Denny Robson (Watts)

Discovering Butterflies and Moths. Keith Porter (Watts)

The Monarch Butterfly. Judith P. Josephson (Crestwood)

Young Naturalist Field Guides (series). (Gareth Stevens)

Videos

Exploring the World of Animals (series). (Library Video)

Insects. (TMW Media)

Look. A Butterfly. (Bullfrog)

Protective Coloration. (Coronet/Multimedia)

Wild Survivors: Camouflage and Mimicry. (National Geographic Society)

Web Sites

mgfx.com/butterfly/

www.bassilichi.it/lorenzi/butterfly/

mgfx.com/butterfly/resource/index.htm

www.sci.mus.mn.us/sln/monarchs/

Index

antennae 10, 15, 21, 28

birdwing 8, 9, 26
blue triangle 5

camouflage 12
caterpillars 4, 6, 7, 8, 9, 10, 11, 12, 13, 14, 20, 24, 25, 29
chrysalis 14, 16, 18, 26, 29
common crow 27, 28
common eggfly 1, 18, 19

eggs 7, 8, 15

eyes 10, 15, 21

green spotted triangle 29

lacewing 12, 16, 17
legs 10, 11

metamor-phosis 14
molting 8, 9
monarch 4, 7, 15, 22, 24, 25, 29
moths 6

names of butterflies (common names) 3, 4, 5
nectar 15, 20, 22

orchard swallowtail 6, 10, 14, 22

painted lady 3, 23
proboscis 20, 21
prolegs 10, 11
pupa 14, 15, 27, 29
purple moonbeam 3

scents 21, 28
skipper 20

tailed emperor 3

Ulysses 11, 29
Union Jack 18, 19

For a free color catalog describing Gareth Stevens Publishing's list of high-quality books and multimedia programs, call 1-800-542-2595 (USA) or 1-800-461-9120 (Canada). Gareth Stevens Publishing's Fax: (414) 225-0377. See our catalog, too, on the World Wide Web: http://gsinc.com

The publisher would like to extend special thanks to Jan W. Rafert, Curator of Primates and Small Mammals, Milwaukee County Zoo, Milwaukee, Wisconsin, for his kind and professional help with the information in this book.

Library of Congress Cataloging-in-Publication Data

Clyne, Densey.
    Flutter by, butterfly / by Densey Clyne.
        p. cm. — (Nature close-ups)
    "First published in 1994 by Allen & Unwin Pty Ltd . . . Australia" — T.p. verso.
    Includes bibliographical references and index.
    Summary: Discusses the life cycle, behavior patterns, and habitats of the exotic beauties of the insect world that undergo a miraculous transformation before earning their wings.
    ISBN 0-8368-2058-4 (lib. bdg.)
    1. Butterflies—Juvenile literature.
[1. Butterflies.] I. Title. II. Series: Clyne, Densey. Nature close-ups.
QL544.2.C59   1998
595.78'9—dc21   97-31736

First published in North America in 1998 by
Gareth Stevens Publishing
1555 North RiverCenter Drive
Suite 201
Milwaukee, WI 53212 USA

First published in 1994 by Allen & Unwin Pty Ltd, 9 Atchison Street, St. Leonards, NSW 2065, Australia. Text and photographs © 1994 by Densey Clyne. Additional end matter © 1998 by Gareth Stevens, Inc.

Printed in the United States of America

1 2 3 4 5 6 7 8 9 02 01 00 99 98